'EQUINE EPITAPH - UNDER THE RAINBOW'

Fraser Island's Last Brumby

FRED WILLIAMS

Balboa Press books may be ordered through booksellers or by contacting:

Balboa Press
A Division of Hay House
1663 Liberty Drive
Bloomington, IN 47403
www.balboapress.com
1 (877) 407-4847

Because of the dynamic nature of the Internet, any web addresses or links contained in this book may have changed since publication and may no longer be valid. The views expressed in this work are solely those of the author and do not necessarily reflect the views of the publisher, and the publisher hereby disclaims any responsibility for them.

Any people depicted in stock imagery provided by Thinkstock are models, and such images are being used for illustrative purposes only.
Certain stock imagery © Thinkstock.

ISBN: 978-1-5043-1176-2 (sc)
ISBN: 978-1-5043-1177-9 (e)

Print information available on the last page.

Balboa Press rev. date: 01/23/2018

BALBOA
PRESS
A DIVISION OF HAY HOUSE

Dedicated to the memories of a fine horseman
William Geissler (alias Billy the Bushman), bushman extraordinaire.
He knew his oranges from his lemons.
Initially employed as a horseman, then finally a ranger;
He contributed massively to our wealth of
Pioneering knowledge on Fraser Island and
Perhaps knew more about the wild horses of Fraser than
Any man that has ever pulled on a pair of boots.

'Billy the Bushman'

FOREWORD

Fred Williams's author of several books on Fraser Island approached me to pen a foreword for his new book titled: **"EQUINE EPITAPH" UNDER THE RAINBOW"** – *Fraser Island's last brumby".*

This is due to my connection with Suffolk Punch horses, having re-introduced the rare and endangered breed back into Australia in 1996. The first foal a filly was born in 2000. Numbers on the ground are still few. This was one of the breeds instrumental in establishing Australia as we know it today.

In reading this book it was a revelation to me that Suffolk Punch horses were introduced along with the Arab breed of horse to Fraser Island in 1879 by the partnership of Aldridge and Dicken. It is not only fascinating but of great importance for Queensland and Australia.

The question is: Where did these Suffolk Punch horses come from and who bred them? Unfortunately we know that Queensland bias/mismanagement sentenced them to death, even after full adaption to cope on the world's largest island of sand. It beggar's belief with a stroke of a bureaucratic pen most were removed or shot.

This book contains factual, sometimes humorous accounts of the people, the animals both domestic and native that enriched their way of life, and how they all harmoniously fitted into the landscape of the island.

You will read of the people living and working at Central Forestry Station. Some were uneducated like "Billy the Bushman" a master craftsman of bushcraft skills employed as horseman for 12 years by the Forestry Department.

The favourite Suffolk Punch horses named *"Nellie* and *Laddie"* as told by Mrs Epps in 1921, as she relates what life was like back then. Fraser Island's Suffolk Punch hoof-prints maybe gone but not forgotten.

Fred Williams in this book brings the traditional owners, residents, foresters and horses back long enough to tell their story. Regrettably they have been replaced with tourists and four wheel drive vehicles. The fragile ecology and landscape has irrefutably been damaged by excessive numbers of visitors, and management seems to be insulated from reality by harsh questionable management plans.

Through the author's words and information, he draws a picture in one's mind of Fraser Island as it used to be, an idyllic lifestyle for some, whilst a harsh extreme environment for others like "Eliza and James Fraser" shipwreck survivors in the year of 1836. But it is a place of great beauty needing protection for the following generations to enjoy, living with nature.

This book gives the reader an enjoyable factual understanding of what an important role Fraser Island is for, its inhabitants, particularly the flora and fauna add this to the loss of the Suffolk Punch and Arab horses (safety role for humans) in Queensland as well as for Australian history. It was a pitiful loss for the preservation of the Suffolk Punch horse breed.

Marge Candy.

P.S. If you hold any information about the Suffolk Punch horses breeding background before Fraser Island. I would appreciate you contacting me at: *suffolkpunchaustralia.com*

A reader poll conducted by *'The Fraser Coast Chronicle'* in September 2016: ***"So far revealed 88% of readers would like to see the brumbies left on Fraser Island..."*** Prior to Queensland Parks and Wildlife Service (QPWS) setting foot on the World's Largest Island of Sand (pre-1971) Fraser Island, was at that time largely unspoiled it was a very special fragile, balanced ecosystem, with 'World-Class' features and unique wilderness. It had many lakes, tragically now it has one less! Lake Yidney was burnt-out by QPWS. Thankfully a range of special beauty spots remain like 'Pile Valley', Central Forestry Station has changed under QPWS, but Bool Creek and Bogimbah areas remain the same to some degree except mango trees planted in 1900's by pioneer Hans Bellert's family were cut down deliberately it seems by QPWS.

One Less Lake. Lake Yidney (forever lost 1992) burnt out under inexperienced QPWS management. The Lake was prior managed by Forestry since 1904. Photo taken by author 1990.

Pile Valley Beauty Spot. Photo by Norma Hannant.

In the rainforest you'll see huge inland trees where ancient cycads grow on pure-sand. The only people who lived and worked there permanently in the 1870's were very early European timber getters and some Aborigines that escaped slaughter in 1851, whose forefathers had stamped their proven historic traditional owner management imprint about 6,000 years ago. They all loved this magnificent paradise. **It was a time before the 'interference' by bureaucrats that this pot of gold existed at the end of the rainbow.** Here are some of those golden nugget memories to ponder over:

Loading Kauri logs onto a log carrier using a bullock team. Shows a mix of European & traditional owners with children. Photo by Richard Daintree State Library of Queensland Circa 1873 (expired copyright)

Impacted rare horse-breed annihilated by QPWS on Fraser Island – Suffolk Punch 5 horse team 1919 (expired copyright) State Library of Queensland.

*Motorised early 'T' model Ford transport on Fraser Island. Note the chains
on the rear wheels. Photo gifted to author by Ruby Jensen.*

Briefly, reflecting back, did you know (not so long ago) before separation from the New South Wales Colony, what is now Brisbane was known as Moreton Bay Convict Penal Settlement 1824 -1842. One of the commandant's was a notorious cruel leader, Commandant Captain Patrick Logan – whose favourite number of punishment lashes with the 'cat-of-nine-tails' was believed to be 500? Ironically, fate intervened and Captain Logan was murdered by his men at 'Logan's Creek' in 1830. In 1837 Brisbane's pioneering family Andrew Petrie arrives in Moreton Bay…His son John became the first Mayor of Brisbane.

*(Monument to Captain Logan). Commandant Patrick Logan's Monument
Plaque. Licensed photo by Brass razoo CC BY-SA 3.0.*

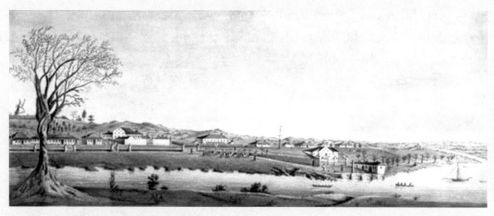

StateLibQld 2 305410 Image of a watercolour painting of Moreton Bay Settlement New South Wales in 1835. Photo State Library of Queensland Creative Commons Attribution-Share Alike 2.5 License.

In 1839 five surveyors were sent from (NSW) to plan the town layout. Dixon, Warner, Stapylton, Tuck and Dunlop (in 1840 Stapylton and Tuck were killed by Aborigines) Dixon controversially returned to Sydney being replaced by Henry Wade in 1841. Wade produced a plan of Brisbane in 1842.

One of the inmates (an escaped convict) in those wild days made it to Fraser Island it seems he had more than his fair share of that ghastly flogging punishment at Moreton Bay Penal settlement. His name was David Bracewell who escaped 7 times and was reluctantly returned discovered on Fraser Island by Pioneer Andrew Petrie in 1842. Bracewell was then employed by Dr Stephen Simpson (Commissioner of Lands) where, ironically and tragically was killed two years later in March 1844 by a falling tree at 'Woogaroo'. Perhaps even worse still was that his 'bad luck' continued even in death it seems, as motorists daily run-over his grave (and other pioneer residents) in Upper Roma Street in Brisbane as the then early graveyard was resumed and built over, becoming a road, it appears, these unmarked graves were not relocated for prosperity.

Brisbane town was later named after Sir Thomas Brisbane the then Governor of the Colony of New South Wales. The new Colony of Queensland separated from New South Wales (NSW) in 1859. Brisbane town was initially laid out with very narrow streets and following-on from that narrow planning and thinking in 1881 Queensland then opted for a narrow gauge railway system against the trend of all other colonies. Nowadays, to bring New South Wales Trains into Brisbane it was necessary to lay a third rail down to accommodate their wider gauge of the (NSW) trains.

In 1870 Pioneer William Pettigrew was Mayor of Brisbane he went into partnership with Robert Sims (earlier around 1863) and constructed a saw mill at Dundathu just outside Maryborough. Pettigrew in September 1863 floated the idea of a tramway on an exploratory trip to Cooroy noting in his diary: *"Tramway could be got past the end of the hill"*. Pettigrew later developed a steam locomotive built by John Walker & Co. of Maryborough that ran on a narrow gauge wooden railway lines to access the milled logs. The engine was self-sufficient, sawing the logs for milling then sawing the railway lines and sleepers to run on, whilst burning the unwanted timber to generate steam power. He named the Engine *'Mary-Ann'* after his daughter. If any readers have any further information about the *'Mary-Ann'* or a later model steam engine named *'Dundathu'* please contact the author c/- the Publisher.

The Mary-Ann on her inaugral day circa 1873. Photo courtesy of Nancy Bates 'Welcome Back Mary-Ann' & Peter Olds - Olds Engineering.

Pettigrew was a member of the Legislative Assembly of Queensland during 1877-94 at the very time when the Queensland Colonial Government adopted the narrow gauge railway system perhaps; Pettigrew's narrow gauge experience may have had considerable influence on the decision. A replica of *'Mary-Ann'* the steam engine was built in 2002 from old photographs by a clever enthusiast engineer Peter Olds at Olds Engine House at Maryborough and runs in the local Botanical Gardens on Thursdays and Sundays.

The Dundathu Mill milled early logs that were rafted across from Fraser Island. Ten years before commercial rail came, the new Colonial Government was struggling along financially and in 1879 with the approval of the new Queensland Colonial Government, two European pioneers Harry Aldridge (the son of the first resident of Maryborough Queensland and George Dicken went into partnership. Aldridge for his part leased two Agricultural pastoral leases on Fraser Island. The *'Indian Head Pastoral lease'*: Extended from Waddy Point to Corroboree Beach and inland to almost half the width of Fraser Island. The area covered 25 square miles and the rental was two pounds sterling per square mile per annum or 50 pounds sterling per year.

'Grouyeah Pastoral Lease': It was believed to be simular in area to Indian Head and rental cost. The lease incorporated land well beyond Lake Boemingen (Now Bubbijin). Therefore, it seems Harry Aldridge paid the Queensland Colonial Government around 100 pounds sterling per year when both leases were in force. In 2014 that would equal a value of about $12,100 to $16,800 Aud.

George Dicken & Wife Mary compliments Constance McDonald.

Harry Aldridge. Photo (expired copyright) State Library of Queensland.

Dicken barged twenty (now endangered horses) including the rare 'Suffolk Punch' and one of the oldest breeds in the world 'Arab' horses along with forty head of cattle transporting them by barge towed by the infamous *'Muriel Bell'* (a steam tugboat) from Susan Creek to the western shores of Fraser Island.

Cattle being barged to Fraser Island. Forestry allowed cattle to graze as a means to control undergrowth. Photo by R&C Schloss.

Dicken began to set up their pioneering homestead camp on the eastern ocean beach (Fraser Island) between Yarong (Eurong) and Lake Wabby. Accompanying them were Aboriginal employees two males Larrikin and Nugget, and two female, Mary and Nora.

On the first night on Fraser Island they heard a long drawn out howl followed by several more. Larrikin raised himself up from his blanket and said: *"Woon-arie, smellum yarraman."* (The wild dogs - dingoes had smelt the horses (yarraman means horse).

Dingo howling. Dingoes do not bark. Photo by Norma Hannant.

Impacted. Thelma rides a legend a rare Suffolk Punch horse Photo compliments Geissler family.

Impacted. Arab horses on Fraser Island. Up to their bellies in fresh water.
Possibly to reduce march flies. Photo compliments Glenda John.

These Government approved (twenty horses) were the first horses ever known in the Island's history to call Fraser Island home. After hearing the wild dingoes' howling, George instructed Nugget and Larrikin to get up quick, whilst they went and checked upon the horses. George slept little that first night and kept one eye open because he could not afford to have these rare and expensive animals attacked, injured or killed.

The next morning they awoke to a chorus of screeching cockatoos and chatter of hundreds of lorikeets including the laconic sound of the Australian kookaburras laughing. (Winding forward, it seems hard to believe that by July of 2001 the extremes of management 'interference' by Queensland Parks and Wildlife Service (QPWS) were on display - shooting native kookaburras at Central Station on Fraser Island.)

The partners created a business plan to develop a unique horse breeding venture partnership, Dicken lived on the island and Harry Aldridge continued living in Maryborough. He negotiated the pastoral leases/runs on Fraser Island from the Queensland Lands Department. Jointly their plan was to cross-breed Arabs over Suffolk Punch horses.

For a copy of the map showing the leased area (see *'Princess K'Gari's Fraser Island – Fraser Island's Definitive History'* by Fred Williams 2002 pp78. You can order a copy <u>mkrail@bigpond.net.au</u>

Both Dicken and Aldridge believed that the horses' progeny would be in high demand locally and also met the set criteria demanded for export markets as gun carriage horses as well as breeding strong cross-breeds suitable for the Indian Army remount program and possibly other theatres of war.

Did you know before the pastoral leases were approved by the supporting Queensland Colonial Government, it ordered a survey of the island to ascertain its **suitability for grazing?** The Government appointed the respected head Botanist Walter Hill of Botanical Gardens in Brisbane to survey Fraser Island as to its suitability for grazing? The Botanical Gardens Botanist gave minimal information in his report but he noted two areas as suitable for grazing, Yarong and Indian Head surrounds, both as it so happens supported blue couch grass. This flowering/seeding couch grass also supported many flocks of Red Browed finches that are now impacted under QPWS.

Impacted. Red browed finches sitting on dead timber. These finches were common when the horses were on Fraser Island because they assisted the blue couch grass to flower and seed. Photo by Norma Hannant.

Thanks to Constance McDonald and family for her story on the *'Fraser Island Run'* (See detail in Williams 2002 pp79). It is not known exactly, just how many horses were bred and exported.

The low-key horse breeding venture would have run a second to the discovery of gold in nearby Gympie (town) in 1867 by pioneer James Nash. At first that township was named Nashville. Nash may have been the first European to massively assist to save Queensland from imminent bankruptcy and perhaps in a smaller way the same could be said of the contribution the horses made when exported to Indian Army from Fraser Island. It raised (huge lease fees) and a tax of one pound per head for the Government. Combined with the early infant logging fees assisted the government coffers. Meanwhile, Fraser Island's importance for its natural resources was slowly expanding.

The commercial narrow gauge Railway did not reach Maryborough until 1881 (3 years after the horse-breeding venture began) and any shipping of horses from the island it seems were trans-shipped by sea at Maryborough and then sent further north to Gladstone port. Here, they were re-loaded again to their destination on specially fitted out long-distance ships with proper accommodation for horses.

Possibly there is another major side to the valuable brumbies that is not widely known or researched: According to Wikipedia:

*The Suffolk Punch …is an English breed of draft horse…from the county of Suffolk in East Anglia. The breed was developed in the early part of the 16th Century. The Suffolk Punch was developed for farm work, and gained popularity during the early 20th century…the breed fell out of favour…and has almost disappeared…the breed's status is **listed as critical by the Rare Breeds Survival Trust…***

Text available under Creative Commons Attribution-ShareAlike License.

About the Arab or Arabian horse according to Wikipedia.

*The Arab horse is a breed of horse that originated on the Arabian Peninsula. With a distinctive head shape and high tail carriage, the Arabian is one of the most easily recognisable horse breeds in the world. It is also **one of the oldest breeds, with archaeological evidence of horses** in the Middle East that resemble modern Arabians dating back 4,500 years…*

Text available under Creative Commons Attribution-ShareAlike Licence.

There were some early beginnings of townships on Fraser Island that began to develop along the eastern beach but they were bark-hut shanties like 'Billy the Bushman's' holiday shack at Yarong and a shack at Yidney built by Captain Marshall Sanderson. The first tourist resort was built at Happy Valley in 1934 (See Williams 2002, pp166). At Yarong there was lots of blue couch grass growing and plots of wild 'pine melon' and a prickly cucumber. The horses used to eat the fruit and spread the seeds in their manure. There were also fields of everlasting daisies growing there, it was a delightful scene to behold.

23 years before QPWS. Marshall Sanderson's shack at Yidney Rocks Circa 1953.
Shack should have been Heritage Listed. Photo by Norma Hannant.

'Be it ever so humble', Geissler's at Yarong holiday shack. Photo Geissler Family Circa 1925.

Jingle bells...Christmas celebration with the Geissler's at Yarong. Photo Geissler Family Circa 1925.

Fraser Island attracted many ship wrecks the most well-known is the rusting hulk, approximately 6-kilometers north of Happy Valley the 5,000 ton TS 'Maheno' washed-up in July 1935 and was stranded on Fraser Island. It was a welcome 'treasure trove' a source for scavenging materials and hosted a wedding ceremony and numerous lovers. Sanderson's heritage shack, boasted teak recycled flooring from the shipwreck along with a range of other souvenirs. Locals in the know including 'Billy the Bushman' would sleep on the ship overnight checking into a first-class cabin and in the morning within the bow of the ship space (now full of sea water) it was possible you could hook a big bream fish for breakfast all without leaving the vessel.

T.S. Maheno, 1935 stranded on the beach during a freak cyclonic storm, whilst being towed to Japan for scrap metal. Photo in collection of Glenda Wilkins.

Happy Valley. First resort 1934. Photo by June & Gordon Elmer.

Love and Romance on the stranded Maheno Circa 1936. Photo by June & Gordon Elmer.

In the centre of the island there was a magnificent area that was so pretty and cool including a sparkling clean creek, lined by piccabeen palms and a rare fern *'Angiopteris Ervecta'* it was like a 'Fairy dell'. Sadly today a walkway has been installed to prevent all those tourists disturbing the roots or transferring disease.

'Woongoolbver' Creek Central Forestry Station Photo by author.

Rare 'Angiopteris Ervecta Fern' Photo by author.

It had the most wonderful unpolluted clear, and fresh water creek with a pure white sandy bottom, called 'Woongoolbver Creek' possibly named after a common plant found on Fraser Island called macrozamia cycad and an infamous dingo you can read about his fascinating and tragic story titled: *"Wangoolba Prince Amongst Dingoes"* 2006 by Fred Williams go to www.Trafford.com order your copy today. The plant's fruit is poisonous, however clever Fraser Island Aborigines discovered a way to consume it by pounding it and soaking it in running water for 3-days before cooking cakes.

Macrozamia Cycad (Wangoolba plant) grows on sand, a poisonous plant (neuro toxins) that the Aborigines discovered how to consume the fruit by pounding it and soaking it in running water for 3-days. Photo by author.

This unique thriving bush town was called Central Forestry Station was the nerve centre of Forestry Operations. Most of the workmen's houses were bark lined, some were a combination of more conventional building materials. One home a Queenslander style was moved there, for use as the island's appointed Foresters' residence. It boasted lovely, cool, shaded and wide verandas all the way around. Cadet Forester Fred Epps and his wife June, described it like this in 1921. (Historic Central Station should have been completely preserved and Heritage Listed, complete with a Museum and the rare Suffolk Punch horses).

'Home sweet home' Billy the Bushman's palace of bark and timber home at Central Forestry Station. Photo Geissler Family.

"Our house consisted of seven large rooms with glorious wide verandas and was situated in one of the most picturesque spots in the centre of the island, 6-miles from both western and eastern beaches. From our kitchen window, you could look down a bank of about 50 feet into a clear and beautiful sandy-bottomed creek with stately palms and fern-bedecked trees on either bank.

Getting ready to survey the Scrub. Note the domesticated dog (left) and Forester's home in background. Photo by Geissler Family.

Down on the creek edge was a little storeroom with shelves in it. In this delightful cool was where the butter was kept to supply all the Forestry folk. Nearby was a motorised water pump that filled our tanks with this lovely fresh clean water supply. Further along was another pretty spot where the children used to bathe. Many times, I took my sewing down there or my afternoon tea and sat and watched the children play. There was a school building of some sorts there during our time. Unfortunately there were not enough children to warrant engaging a teacher. The children hardly knew what to do with themselves so I used to give them books and papers to read.

Elkhorn and hares foot fern grew abundantly all around and it seemed all-year-round some tree or shrub was bearing fruit or sweet smelling flowers. In the spring particularly: the island was one of mass flowers: – Christmas bells, Boronia, acacia our home was always decorated with blooms.

Christmas Bells. Exquisite like a Swiss Designed Timepiece and yet beautifully delicate flowering plant on Fraser Island. Photo by Norma Hannant.

Another front-line erosion fighting plant Goats Foot found on the first sand dunes on Fraser. Note how the plant deflects the moving sand in its fan-shaped leaves. Photo by author.

Birds of every kind and colour sang in the shrubs close to the house". (Due to blue couch grass many of these birds like the vast flocks of Finches are now missing impacted on Fraser Island.) "Timid wallabies" (also missing impacted) "sometimes they played in the plantation in front of our home and goannas would boldly crawl up on the back steps to the kitchen during the day looking for food. At night the possums used to visit us and have their meal from the scrap tin. They were so pretty and shy. We never saw any snakes" (also many have been impacted) "all the three years we lived on the island.

Fraser Island's deadliest killer. Ted Roachford holds a dead death Adder
Snake killed at Central Station 1925. Photo Geissler Family.

Pretty Faced Wallaby at Cathedral Beach Resort. Now Impacted. They were brown
in colour here yet grey in other parts of the island. Photo by Norma Hannant.

The Epps's Queenslander style home in background. Getting ready to ride out into the scrub. Photo Compliments June Hunt.

Our mail came only once a fortnight and so when the newspapers arrived we read of the troubles and sorrows of the world. It seemed like old news and did not worry us. Indeed, we seemed to live for the present. No one ever appeared to be suffering from sickness. Sometimes, someone would bring influenza back from town, but it soon left them. Who wouldn't be happy and healthy living in such a wonderful part of the world like Fraser Island?

Very often I went out with my husband, riding round and about the scrub where he attended his business with the Forestry men and some timber-getters at the various camps. I was never bored since I did all my home duties myself. I made all our bread, jam, pickles and chutneys.

We had many delightful picnics and drives to the main beach. Two or three big strong horses would be put in the spring-cart. We would load it up with eats and climb aboard. Then away we would drive along the sandy tracks through the shady canopy and dense scrub. If we had visitors we would stop and give our visitors the experience of drinking from the marvellous water vine, which hung from the canopy like swings, that I believe was a wonderful piece of Nature's handy-work on Fraser Island.

Indian Head from the air. Photo by Norma Hannant.

Andrew Postan demonstrates the 'Water Vine' Photo by author.

One Christmas, Eppsie (my husband's nick-name) we set off alone on a camping trip to Indian Head. We took the spring-cart loaded up with plenty of horse-feed like: mixed-up oat and Lucerne chaff, pollard, corn and bread when available. The animals ate about a 20 litre container each per day.

On Route to one of our Picnics. Photo Compliments June Hunt.

Water was created at our camp easily by digging a hole in the sand. The horses all had names like, Snip, Bully, Nellie, Mega, Laddie and Kim. We chose out of ten animals, two big strong horses. Our favourites were Laddie and Nellie. We loaded up plenty of Christmas delicacies supplies for ourselves.

In December it was very hot on the beach so we rested during the day and travelled at night. The horses were quite frightened at the sound of the waves crashing on the beach. Many times six or seven wild horses galloped up to us, stared and snorted at us before careering away, only to follow us for miles at a safe distance. It was a strange feeling driving at night on that lonely moon-lit beach with the terrific generated noise of the ocean and the wind.

Before QPWS bias interfered. Wild horses at Yidney Rocks Circa 1953. Photo by Norma Hannant.

When we reached Indian Head, Eppsie soon had a sweet little camp prepared for us. He pitched a fly (sheet of canvas) from the cart to a few trees" (obviously the dingoes were not starving then or attacking or causing problems and there was no fenced off areas prior to QPWS management in 1971, the dingoes then were contented and hunted only at night. As long as the brumbies existed humans were safe).

"We carried some big cedar boards up from the beach to our camp that were washed-up on the beach to make a rough bush table. Packing cases were likewise found on the beach that provided as a make-do cupboard and a pantry. We gathered an abundance of leaves to put under our mattress and soon had a comfy bed.

Just a short distance outside the camp, at the foot of a green hill, Eppsie dug a hole and out sprang lovely fresh clean drinkable water that we and the horses utilised all the time we were camping. Our bread soon became mouldy, so we made good damper and feasted on the great fat oysters and crabs which were most plentiful" (now impacted) "that we could collect at low tide around the rock base of Indian Head in those days.

In 1922, our little daughter was born. June was a beautiful baby, rosy- cheeked, golden haired and healthy. She never had any ailments – just grew and grew and was no trouble. This was just as well since there was no woman on the island I could converse with about babies.

Just nearby to our home at Central Forestry Station was a huge plant nursery, it was built by Forestry to grow young forestry tree seedlings. Thanks to the flocks of cockatoos" (that ate the seed in the cones and many times bit the seed cones clean off) "we collected these fallen Kauri cones and dried the seed for export to the U.S. In the early days our supplies, letters and parcels were all brought here from the boat/s that used to come from Maryborough and would moor in Wangoolbver Creek. Special thanks to June Hunt for sharing their wonderful memories about Fraser Island (Reproduced from 'Written in Sand-A History of Fraser Island' with permission of the author).

Forestry. Tree seedling nursery. Photo Geissler Family.

The only way to town in 1925 was via Suffolk Punch horse and cart. Photo by Geissler family.

I want you to meet one of Fraser Island's most outstanding and unique characters that ever pulled on a pair of boots on the island. He was a natural, blessed with an encyclopaedic understanding about all-things Fraser Island. 'Billy the Bushman' alias William Geissler lived there in the wilds of Fraser Island bush at Central Forestry Station in 1925 with his wife and family a year after the Epps's left. He was employed by the Forestry Department as a horse breaker, Forestry also managed the island and commercial logging on Fraser Island.

'Billy the Bushman's' bushcraft skills and vast knowledge was invaluable he was multi-talented, his schooling perhaps was limited as he had been raised under the school of hard knocks – but his vast experience was wide-ranging, a guide, bush carpenter, a horse breaker with an in-depth understanding of horses, road builder, fire-break expert, supervisor foreman, naturalist, amateur ecologist and botanist even photographer was amongst his wide range of bushcraft skills. He also transported the dedicated school building into Central Station on a horse lorry with six horses. Most of all he greatly admired the magnificent wild brumby. He reckons the Suffolk Punch Horse was rarer than rocking horse droppings or hens teeth. Could you imagine in the same class of rarity as world class China's Giant Panda or the Siberian Tiger?

'Billy The Bushman' and Family. Photo Geissler Family.

School House moved by 'Billy the Bushman' using six horses and a dray. Photo Geissler Family.

Modified, many years later school house converted to Forestry Information Center. Note the trees bedecked with elkhorn fern planted by 'Billy the Bushman'. Photo by Norma Hannant.

He espoused the belief in people would come from miles around just to appreciate or see one of the Suffolk Punch horses working. They were so quiet and had gentle natures. He also showed concern about signs of the changing environment i.e. the dropping numbers of sea snakes being washed-up on Fraser Island and saw it as a worrying sign of the state of health of the ocean. As he had access to the use of the facilities of the nursery he grew lots of seedlings including guava trees, cherry and yellow, planted orange, mandarin and lemon trees including the bush lemon particularly around Yankee Jack Creek, Panama Creek, and Wangoolbver Creek. He also planted a vast number of passionfruit vines. Other edible wild plants grew all around like pine melons used for jam making and prickly cucumber. "A ripe melon weighing over 60.5 pounds" was reported by (Maryborough Chronicle 1929).

A distant view of the Forester-in-charge home at Central Station. Photo Geissler family.

Noel Mathison in 1999 shows off a lemon tree most likely planted by 'Billy the Bushman' Photo by author.

"Billy the Bushman' reckoned there were vast flocks of finches (due to blue couch grass) and other birds living and breeding around Central Forestry Station. Billy the Bushman's family lived there during the entire time of his appointment. There was no shop handy to patronise to get insect repellent, potting mix or garden supplies. One-day 'Billy the Bushman' captured a pair of bush stone-curlews that are now impacted (at Central) and placed them into their fenced home vegetable patch to keep the grubs and other insects under control.

'Billy the Bushman' says the children knew nothing of the birds being captured and relocated into that fenced vegetable patch. Until one day they sneaked in to nick a few peas and beans from the veggie-patch to substitute their diet and guess what, they got quite a fright when the curlews suddenly appeared. He also had wild fowls on the island but they reckon you had to get-up exceptionally early to collect an egg as the pythons and goannas were connoisseurs, great lovers of eggs.

Bush Stone-Curlew Egg Nest. Photo by Norma Hannant.

You had to get up early to collect an egg. Wild fowls belonging to 'Billy the Bushman'. Photo by Geissler Family.

According to 'Billy the Bushman' son one of the horse paddocks that he had fenced had been nick-named 'The Ghost Paddock' due to its bare patches of sand in-between the clumps of blue couch and spinifex grass. A strong viable population of one of Australia's endemic iconic ground-dwelling birds the bush stone-curlews occupied this area. The curlews were observed by two pioneering families (Geissler's circa 1925 and the Bellert's circa 1930's). The Ghost paddock was so named because of those bare patches of sand and the birds congregated there and often when the clouds passed overhead it cast long or short shadows of different shapes and sizes. It had an eerie ghostly-like feel and appearance. From reports the Aborigines at Central Station were terrified of this horse paddock.

'Billy the Bushman' noticed when the curlews laid their eggs in their ground nests they were in very roughly constructed nests, mainly a few twigs and leaves. Just after being laid, the egg shells blotched like magic with the colours of their surrounds to give them camouflage. The birds incubated the eggs spasmodically as required until the chicks hatched. According to Wikipedia: *"It is mainly nocturnal and specialises in hunting small grassland animals: frogs, spiders, insects, molluscs, crustaceans, snakes lizards and small mammals are all taken, mostly gleaned or probed from soft soil or rotting wood…Birds usually forage individually or in pairs over a large home range, particularly on moonlit nights…The bush stone curlew is probably heard more than it is seen. Its call sounds like a wail or a scream in the night…"*

Heard more than it is seen. Bush Stone curlew Impacted from Central Station area, small population on Western side of Island. Photo by Norma Hannant.

'Billy the Bushman' on behalf of his employer the Forestry Department was instructed to capture some of the brumbies so that they could be broken-in for riding. Many times to capture them he would send 'Banjo' an Aboriginal and his friend 'Willy' or Brother 'Ike' to chase some of the wild horses onto the beach often up as far as Indian Head.

Then, 'Billy the Bushman' would chase them south down along the beach. Occasionally the animals veered-off and went into the surf. His son 'Bill the Farouk' said he saw his father swim out after a horse one-day and grab hold of the tail and then get on the back of the wild brumby and ride it to shore. Usually such horse behaviour tired the animal out and it was then more easily driven along to Yarong or Central Station.

impacted. Some of the Suffolk Punch cross breeds. Wild horses at Orchid Beach grazing. Photo compliments Glenda John.

'Billy the bushman' employed as a horse-breaker by Forestry Department 1925-1937. Breaking in a brumby. Photo by Geissler Family.

Breaking-in the magnificent brumbies for use as riding horses in
Forestry operations 1925-1937. Photo by Geissler family.

But first of all to hold these wild horses he had to build strong fenced yards to retain the captured horses. The first yard built was at Yarong and the second on the other side of Wangoolbver Creek. 'Billy the Bushman' planted some sweet grasses for the horses to eat. He also put down spears, so the developing plants could be kept moist.

Some of the other workers harnessed up the heavy work horses to a dray placing the newest broken-in ones in the shafts and the others were placed as leaders and they headed to the eastern beach some hour and a half away.

The plan was to dig-up and harvest a quantity of spinifex grass runners, the male plants have runners and the females throw seed that can be seen at times cartwheeling along the beach in strong winds.

Cartwheeling seeds, Another amazing sand dune plant. The female
spinifex grass seeds (maturing). Photo by Norma Hannant.

From selected frontal sand dunes male spinifex runners were collected along with some blue couch grass runners from Yarong. The workers stayed for almost a full day and got quite a load of runners to transplant. They tied them down and then returned home to Central Station.

The next day as daylight broke though the surrounding green canopy they went into the paddock on the other-side of the creek that was in the process of being fenced by another work-gang of men under his supervision.

They unloaded the runners, spreading them all around the paddock. Some of the men with axes chopped-up the long runners into manageable pieces. Other workmen came along and planted one end into the sandy soil. It was a naturally moist area being near the creek and the spinifex and couch grass runners soon struck and began growing in their new home. Some rails were placed in the fence line along the creek side so that it could be opened easily to let the horses swim and drink there from time to time.

The horse paddock was replicated at Yarong adding spinifex runners to the blue couch grass and soon both paddocks were completed. About two months later the spinifex grass was growing tall. A spear was put down into the sand for water to keep the areas moist and growing. Over time other native grasses were also transplanted to give the horses some variety.

'Billy the Bushman' has a soft spot for the Yarong area (now called Eurong) as well as Central Forestry Station. So much so that he built a rough bush shack there for the family to holiday. The family went there sometimes in company of other families for Christmas, birthdays and other special occasions. It offered good fishing and Billy the bushman was known to have ridden his bicycle to the TS Maheno stranded on the beach past Happy Valley.

The next task to undertake was to capture for breaking-in some of Fraser Island's magnificent wild horses. 'Billy the Bushman' was instructed to capture fine looking specimens for riding horses and Suffolk Punches with heavier build as work horses. The problem with a wild mob when mustered – or chased, the mares would always follow the stallion, so the stallion was targeted, isolated or at worst removed.

Then they would bring in quieter broken horses for the mares to follow and the men riding horses were then able to eventually turn or push or guide the mob into the pre-prepared paddocks. Many of the mares had foals a foot and care was needed as sometimes they can be harmed in a chase or round-up or mustering.

Out of the chase round-up came some very fine specimens and the next task was to break-in these horses. 'Billy the Bushman' would tie them up to a long line so they could get used to a halter and being fed and handled. He was skilled in this area, he named the horses and along with a work-mate they began the process of riding, handling and breaking-in the horses to gain their confidence. The first two weeks of training was fairly tough. The breaking-in process was no easy task and could take several weeks of intensive attention, care and training. You could easily get badly hurt or thrown off a bucking horse. There were no hospitals or doctors nearby but perhaps one-thing in their favour was the sand was soft.

Impacted Wild Horse. 'Bully the Brumby' ridden by Bert Roots Circa 1930's. Photo by Geissler family.

One outstanding brumby was 'bully the brumby': he was a horse belonging to Bert Roots a timber getter. He was a very fine horse and Bert was very proud of him. He rode him everywhere on the island.

Any horses that did not meet the strict criteria of 'Billy the Bushman' were released and more were recaptured and broken-in until he located the high standard of horses required. Some of these horses had adapted very well to the sandy conditions and their feet were splayed so that they left little imprint in the sand to start erosion. Their feet hit the sand flatfooted so that they didn't scoop out the sand like other mainland horses.

Mother Nature was in-charge her population control was two-fold. On one hand some horses suffered from sand colic through ingesting sand with their food then on the other dingoes culled the animals. Sand colic shortened their lives considerably from around 35 years to 9 years. The foals, the old and the sick or weak were easily preyed upon by dingoes. Dingoes at that time hunted in packs to bring the horses down and consumed the high protein meat, rich in trace elements and minerals so long as the brumbies remained the prey of the dingo it was safe for humans. Did you know 'Billy the Bushman' understood the fine threads of balance and harmony between predator and prey but it seems few folks understood that on Fraser Island it was because of the wild horses running free - that humans enjoyed dingo safety?

It was a very sad day indeed for the World's Largest Island of Sand when 'Billy the Bushman' eventually left Fraser Island in 1937. He was transferred and went to another area. Fraser Island lost a vital key-stone quintessential old-school and master bushman extraordinaire and advisor – who held a real thorough and complete understanding of Fraser Island. It was a loss that came at a catastrophic high price it seems – sadly his knowledge-base after he left was (where the start of all the troubles began). This knowledge-base has never been replaced on the World's Largest Island of Sand!

Winding the clock back a little further during the 'Great depression' 1930-1939 Queensland along with the rest of the Australian people suffered badly. In 1930's three joint enterprising owners of some freehold land on the west coast of Fraser Island McLiver, Bagnall and Woods harvested excess brumbies, rounding them-up, driving them (called mustering) to Wathumba Creek pushing them into temporary yards. It is believed retired sergeant Tom King was very keen to get back into the saddle, putting his hand-up to participate in this muster and sadly most unexpectedly died. It is believed he took a heart attack at Wathumba and his body was taken back in a boat the 'Woodford' borrowed from Hans Bellert at Bogimbah by Ike Owens. See *'Princess K'Gari's Fraser Island – Fraser Island's Definitive History'* Obtain your copy *mkrail@bigpondpond.net.au*

Sergeant Tom King. Renowned for his Fists of Iron. Photo compliments Hervey Bay Historical Village & Museum.

These mustered horses were then punted to the mainland in a barge towed by Bendy Webber's punt, where they were yarded and the horses sold –off at between thirty to sixty shillings per head (three to six dollars) according to Ike Owens (See Williams *'Princess K'Gari's Fraser Island' - Fraser Island's Definitive History.* 2002).

In 1939 WWII broke out and Forestry operations were wound back accordingly. The first of two training schools in October 1943 of the Z-Force of the Australian Army began at McKenzie's old sawmill site and later at Lake McKenzie. They drew on Forestry for the horses they needed (exact numbers unknown). (See *'Princess K'Gari's Fraser Island'* 2002 pp185-188 by Fred Williams for the details.)

Z Force. Tatical Relief model. Map of Singapore Harbour constructed of concrete. Photo by author.

Z Force. Tactical Relief model plaque used in training camp 1943.
Plaque stolen under QPWS management. Photo by author.

Things were changing fast on Fraser Island by 1971. The Queensland Parks and Wildlife Service (QPWS) first set foot on the place (without appointing any equal to 'Billy the Bushman') and were appointed by the Queensland Government to manage the first National Park on the northern end of Fraser Island – troubles began from the first footprint as they 'interfered' in lieu of 'conserving'.

One of the obvious problems they were totally inexperienced bureaucratic and academic style managers possibly they were schooled in the theory but not the practical (the opposite of 'Billy the Bushman'- not hands–on, salt-of-the- earth folks to guide and direct them by practical experience) and it seems from what we now know, they did not have any practical horsemen employed to help them **'understand Fraser Island'** where it was the home of some rare important wild horses, yet according to the QPWS's submission to the 'Joint Committee of Managers' claimed in 1978:" *The natural resources of the national park is by no means yet fully understood..."* no advisor foreman/ supervising manager like the skilled knowledge and understanding of 'Billy the Bushman' (who graduated from the school of hard knocks). Troubles began over <u>understanding</u>'!

They also seemed to be suffering from a bureaucratic *'helpless inability'* or possibly were distracted by this unique island experience as recorded by the experienced pioneers who knew what it was to do a hard day's work and did not wear a uniform or a shirt with epaulets, long socks or nice shiny black boots.

From the outside looking-in the rangers and managers employed in the service it seems acted like they were 'Officers in Charge', there appeared to be an apparent lack of expertise at the coal-face or grass-roots level, they demonstrated that they even lacked machinery operating skills with their grader operations. Instead, they penned multiple numbers of 'academic or bureaucratic management plans' began hatching the first of what grew to be a series or forest of management strategies/plans for the Island, sometimes recording promises, it seems but adamantly believed they were always right - finding it difficult to accept community advice or answer criticism or enter into great partnerships and followed their own bureaucratic assumptions or conclusions - made without the benefit of essential knowledge of a 'Billy the Bushman' type or equal to a head ranger in charge. A good example of this essential short-fall in the knowledge-base appeared in the public forum just 2-years into QPWS's appointment to manage the first National Park. It signalled a looming catastrophic change it was delivered by a new Department (with no managerial experience on Fraser Island whatsoever) who perhaps with respect would not know one end of the horse from the other. A newspaper article published in the *'Sunday Mail'* November 18, 1973: Head Lines were: ***"ISLAND HORSES MAY GO"*** *Fraser Island's wild horses may end up in the knackery.*

It was a tragic beginning for the island that required a 'highly skilled' and 'Innovative Manager'. In 1978 the Queensland Government that was also equally unskilled at managing Fraser Island appointed a complex conglomerate a mix-mash of government departments to manage the island. A new department was created and appointed like the Beach Protection Authority (BPA). It created a management mess!

It seems also the BPA had no prior 'on the ground' managerial experience whatsoever on Fraser Island (no 'Billy the Bushman' bushcraft skilled horsemen either) these complexities offered floor to ceiling academics and engineers. Nil expertise at the coal-face with Fraser Island brumbies or long history of moving sands and erosion or cattle grazing, fighting wildfires or managing the under-story of the forest to keep the growth down or knew how to cut a fire-break using a 'delva or grader' pulled by horses to reduce fire risk and cope with lightning strikes.

It was in the author's mind a total and utter disaster to think that this was going to be regarded as an innovative workable plan to manage and enhance this wilderness area a fragile harmonious, balanced ecosystem. Going back to that newspaper article of November 18, 1973 this brand-new department on the block was the Beach Protection Authority (BPA) they showed their total bias hand in this article published in the Sunday Mail <u>5-years before they were even appointed to head up recommendations</u> (it beggars belief) <u>to the joint Fraser Island management committee.</u> Their bias towards the brumbies was made crystal clear the authorities chief Engineer said: *"They could be shot; rounded up and taken to the mainland knackery; or stallions could be sterilised…He anticipates there could be an outcry against any removal of the horses…"* BPA it seems followed calls being made by some Forestry (Graziers) leaseholders to have the area brumby free. (Daily Mercury 1947).

Grazing the tough spinifex Grass, Fraser Island's valuable brumbies 'wild & free' under Forestry 1904-1978. Photo taken Circa 1958. Hervey Bay Historical Village & Museum.

In the first of this forest of Fraser Island Management Plans ever produced on the island by European Queensland Government managers such plans were created it seems by utilizing unqualified in-house QPWS staff (totally inexperienced in managing Fraser Island) and submissions were written and lodged by all the various departments to the *'Joint Committee of Management'* (May 1978) submissions that would perhaps guarantee to make 'Billy the Bushman' turn over in his grave according to Wikipedia: *"It is also said of deceased founder(s)…if their extant leadership goes against the founder(s)'principles…"*

Bias plans came from managers to destroy, kill and interfere when most folks were expecting the opposite that these managers should have been nurturing and caring. Managers' bias claims surfaced about the horses that were Mother Nature's healers, came without full transparency, public interest or scrutiny or consultation. QPWS authors did not consult the grass roots surviving family of 'Billy the Bushman'. Instead, of looking to conserve these valuable horses like has been done on Assateague Island by the U S National Parks Service (NPS) since 1965. Their bias submission in 1978 claimed:

*"**Feral horses** are the most significant feral species on the national park…it is a widely held view that feral animals cannot be permitted in national parks…"*

NOTE: Such a widely held view was in fact it seems the manager's view. It was not a view embraced by the community. QPWS always referred to the horses as 'FERAL' never as 'Wild horses'.

It appears departmental managers failed to conduct a thorough comprehensive in-depth study into the rare endangered Suffolk Punch horses. As well as the historic Arab horses used to commence or the **first Government approved breeding venture on Fraser Island** where the **'grazing runs'** had also been approved by the Queensland Lands Department and recommended by the chief biologist of the Botanical Gardens.

As a consequence of QPWS ideas a 'turn-coat' bias views were adopted (opposing the horses 'Lest we Forget') they failed to take-in the vast 'public interest' and in the process underestimated the intense interest or their obligatory duty of care to discover the status of these historic rare Suffolk Punch horses that were listed as critically endangered by experts. The Suffolk Punch was a declining breed and that the concept of what the progeny was designed and bred for as gun-carriage horses and Army remounts was also very important and formed a part of unique heritage in Queensland history. The horses were a real special part of Queensland colonial history on Fraser Island and would have been of tremendous on-going historical interest and enjoyment, to meet a demand of world-wide attraction of lovers of horses. For information on Suffolk Punches go to *www.suffolkpunchaustralia.com*

Samford Jack, founding stallion of modern day Australian Suffolk Punches in his shaded gum-tree paddock, Inverell N.S.W. compliments Marge Candy www.suffolkpunchaustralia.com

It can be done in the U.S. but not on Fraser Island.Wild ponies on Assateague Island. NPS in the US have been successfully managing horses since 1965. Photo by dreamstime_xl_25607078 RF Licence.

A WORLD APART - TWO OPPOSING MANAGEMENT PLANS.

Since 1965 on opposite sides of the world for example: Assateague Island horses were being managed successfully, signs were erected warning visitors not to approach of feed wild horses as they can kick and bite, charge and knock people down –fines apply.

DOWN UNDER DUE TO A TOURISM AGENDA (1985) THE HORSES WERE SACRIFICED –THEN DINGOES THAT HAD A 6,000+ YEAR SAFETY RECORD AROUND HUMANS SLOWLY BEGAN TO STARVE, EMACIATE AND ATTACK HUMANS.

Reflecting back to 1851 (8-years before Queensland separated) where a European Magistrate E.B. Uhr based in Maryborough asked the New South Wales Colonial Government to provide the Native Police Corps under a European Commandant to raid Fraser Island. From reports the Aborigines were viciously murdered and slaughtered. Then by 1860's early European timber extraction resources began to flow to the saw-mills of Maryborough Queensland. The timber targeted was softwoods so that they could raft the logs across the sea (using tides) and up the river to the mills. Management plans related solely to forestry management.

A raft of changes, enter Queensland Parks and Wildlife (QPWS) to Fraser Island Management scene in 1971 with the appointment to manage the first (Northern end) National Park.

In just 7-years things began to change. By1978 the QPWS with respect (as a totally inexperienced manager) began developing the first (Fraser Island Management Plan) that could be described as the beginning in a series of a vast 'FOREST' of management plans.

LIKE ASSATEAGUE, ON FRASER ISLAND VISITORS WERE WARNED NOT TO FEED WILDLIFE AND THAT DINGOES COULD ATTACK, BITE AND INJURY. **BUT HERE'S THE DIFFERENT THING** - BY 2001 THEIR TRAGIC HARSH MANAGEMENT PLAN CHANGES REVEALED **DINGOES CAN KILL HUMANS a (big difference).**

At the time there appeared to be two opposing strategies of management? The Forestry Department (under the *'Conservator of Forests'*) managing timber extraction and controlled undergrowth including grazing, fire, fire-breaks and lightning strikes and maintenance in the forest. Forestry at the time employed seven rangers to manage tourism and other forestry related business.

Then on the opposing benches was the emergence of this conglomerate or a mix-mash of State Government Departments (all inexperienced on managing Fraser Island) appointed a *'Joint Committee of Management'* and then strange as it may seem bureaucrats then appointed the newest State Department the Beach Protection Authority (BPA) that made recommendations on behalf of all involved to report to the (above committee).

BPA's strategy concentrated on alleged erosion by horses (on an island that was built on moving grains of sand) blaming erosion solely on the horses, totally ignoring (the consequences) if horses were removed, also ignored the domino effect upon the wild dogs (top predator and a carnivore) would be horrific by withdrawing access to their key prey, a high protein food resource (like the old, sick, the weak and foals) introducing totally unheard of before strategies of environmental dislocation upon the balanced, harmonious ecosystem. Their plan didn't provide for any equal replacement food resources.

By introducing this controversial management plan it resulted in interference with dingoes cardinal food-web resources – combined with slowly switching strategies from timber harvesting to strategies of high impact Tourism by encouraging large numbers of visitors, causing escalating dislocation. Tourism numbers had no ceiling.

To assist with inviting tourists it was convenient at that time it seems to piggy-back on the *'Fraser Island Defenders Organisation'* (FIDO) emergence to continue their intensive protesting about Sand-Mining Operations and efforts to promote Fraser Island tourism. It however, came at a cost as FIDO utilised these visitors to increase their membership numbers and to raise finances.

Early management according to one local veteran surgeon if he is right was hired to start the plan by controlling the stallions with sterilising, (a process it seems some stallions do not survive well) as well as killing and removal.

As sand and time flowed down the hour glass after 1992 when the QPWS were appointed to manage the whole island (and the island additionally won World Heritage status) new instalments were made on management plans that targeted authority to kill dingoes 'without notice' and a range of fines options for feeding.

QPWS began their killing spree (whole dingo pack of 14+ killed at Happy Valley 1994) and killed/removed horses from Eli Creek to Indian Head according to pioneer resident Norma Hannant. However, this important issue of brumby bias (that we have only just touched on here; it seems was the trigger that (we are now all beginning to understand had dire consequences.) Horses provided safety for humans around dingoes since 1879. It may not yet be finished) – the next chapter in the horse saga has yet to be penned on Fraser Island.

Poor Quality Photo. Secretly built rough horse trap erected at rear of Eurong Resort 1991. Designed to capture horses. Photo by Sonia Hutchinson.

In a recent discovery via a camera trap set by QPWS's on the western side of the island seven mares and a stallion were discovered living harmoniously. It is not known if this mob is yet large enough to be able to save humans from further attacks. Now suddenly as the news broke in the community - that **stallion has gone missing!** Did this stallion meet the same cruel deathly 'interference' fate, at the hands of the QPWS management or can you suggest or do you know what has happened to that stallion? What is the solution for managing this precious Fraser Island that is in crisis under the arc of the rainbow?

INVITATION TO YOU

We invite you and would welcome your comments especially any U S residents who have visited Assateague Island or Cumberland Georgia or any other areas where National Parks Service (NPS) manage wild horses successfully.

'Skeletons that rattle' a disgrace to QPWS bureaucratic bias strategies. Photo by author.

Mighty tough finding food as a top predator food became a curly situation on Fraser Island under QPWS, photo gifted to author by Easy Four-Wheel drives Rainbow Beach.

Impacted. Brumby foal in the care of mother's watchful eye. Photo by Norma Hannant.

Email the author with your thoughts to the author's domain web-site www.Kgari.org where it will be published (if content is suitable) to share with the interested Australian community.

Whatever your view, we would like to hear from you including any photographs with your kind permission to use them. **<u>To my mind the removal or interference with horses on Fraser Island created the greatest upset to the fragile harmonious balanced ecosystem food-web ever known - in the entire history of Fraser Island and in particular given the detrimental domino effect that triggered the loss and tragedy of human safety around dingoes.</u>** It is claimed by experts that if you interfere with just one (from tiny ants) in the ecosystem - one species or another is affected and so a chain reaction is created.

Around the same time Lyall Sempf of Brumby Watch Australia and Aboriginal Elder John Dalungdalee Jones claimed: Under Native Title and associated rights was vigorously protesting about the illegal removal of the brumbies by QPWS. Further they jointly claim: *"Nothing in the Great Sandy Management Plan of 1994 is intended to diminish or extinguish native title and associated rights"*

The Queensland Government 100% denied their genuine claim even though Elder Jones had secured an order from the court (Justice Shepherdson in July 1997) to represent 22 elders of the Aboriginal family groups, Ngulungbara, Batjala and Dalungbara peoples of Fraser Island and Wide Bay area. Queensland's arrogant approach towards authorised traditional owners should be carefully noted.

It seems that another party who aided their removal was John Sinclair of Fraser Island Defender's Organisation (F.I.D.O) he came up with an unverifiable spurious spin suggestion that the horses were destroying the Pandanus Palms shoots and ecosystem, by citing a bogus reference allegedly from history attributing the quote to pioneer Forester Walter Petrie 1913. It was highly questionable piece of spin especially when the wild horses always resided on the eastern beach where the sweet blue couch and spinifex grass grew. Although F.I.D.O supported the Government's position it turned out that the self-appointed 'watchdog' F.I.D.O actually fractured the views of those that most likely support the group. It seems the massive majority outcry and views from the 'public interest' were ignored.

It appears also there are no winners in the brumby debate with the perpetrator being the Queensland Government and its overarching Department of Environment (DERM), it appears it has reaped the consequences and inherited all the on-going problems over the bureaucratic removal and killing strategy (by not developing a practical solution from someone like experienced horseman 'Billy the Bushman'.) Instead what was delivered was a domino 'interfering' strategies that followed like starving dingoes for their high protein food resource without providing any equivalent replacement resource.

It proved to be a horrific down-side for tourism/visitor agenda as attacks and injuries began to occur with uncontrollable rapidity on this sandy paradise. Emaciated dingoes began appearing for the first time in the memory of pioneers. If radio interviews aired on the ABC network are right, the Community it seems have lost faith and become hostile and most intolerant towards DERM and QPWS.

Emaciated dingo with just hours to live – starved to death by unacceptable deprivation of food resource strategies under QPWS. Photo Norma Hannant.

Dingo behaviour changes combined with strategies to reduce numbers of dingoes appeared in another plan (dFIDMS 1999) in hand with the concept of promoting excessive tourism by bureaucrats to turn Fraser Island into a Tourist clone of Surfers Paradise according to the Minister of Tourism Peter McKechnie (Overlander 1985).

In no time the vast people problem (for dollars) turned catastrophic as the visiting numbers rose to unacceptable levels. The QPWS strategy had the effect of swamping the island with over 500,000+ visitors per annum and rising. Verses limited balanced tourism (say of under 20,000 visitors per annum that were known during the early 1970's).

Tourism on Fraser, an agenda of the Tourism Minister (1985) packed like commuters on a bus. Photo in collection of author.

Management strategies need to be exchanged to another model like under a proven active board of traditional owner management to protect what's left of a once special unique wilderness and home of the last pure bred dingoes in all Queensland (maybe the world). A declared World Heritage Area and the World's largest Island of Sand, all features which have plagued the controversial (dollar chasing) academic management style of QPWS over the last 2.5 decades until today and rising. It is claimed that over 500 visitors have been attacked by dingoes over these last 25 years under QPWS management and one death recorded. Camping can have grave risks.

Where it appears the expansive vision by bureaucrats of inviting unlimited numbers of visitors have been to specifically raise funds for what we believe are harsh enforcement management plans. The record shows ever since QPWS stepped onto this island the price apart from the access fees is being paid not only from the wallet but in human blood, trauma, pain, tragedy and even death. Whilst rare critically endangered Suffolk Punch Cross breed horses were deliberately annihilated as well their special historic progeny.

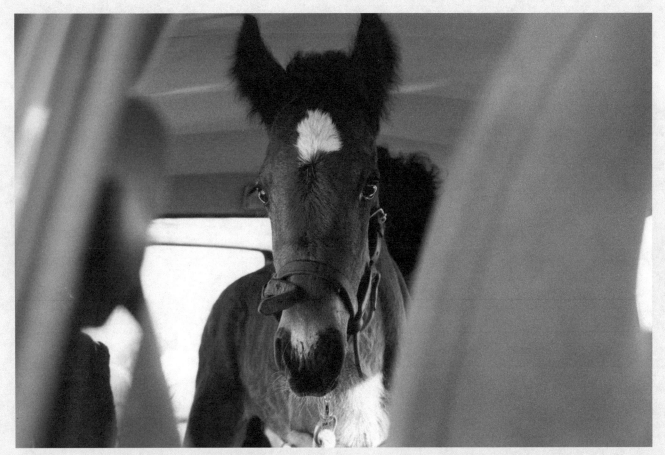

'Ellie' a few days old, looking out the back window of the Pajero at her new world without her mother. Photo compliments Sonia Hutchinson.

ELLIE'S ESCAPE FROM THE CLUTCHES OF QPWS

On one high drama filled day in November 1997 just after the first critical 48 hours of a newly born foal's life the dire need was for the foal to enjoy the security of its mother. This lone foal was discovered on Ellie's Track at Orchid Beach being attacked by dingoes. She had been bitten on the back and the little animal was totally defenceless, all alone in the world and shaking on her terrified little wobbly legs. Her mother was under attack had to bolt-off terrified, leaving her little new-born foal behind, just to escape with her own life.

Her foal was left all alone in the world and faced certain death as the dingoes begun attacking their prey. Luckily, the local folks came to her rescue that lived nearby and took her back to their home and locked her safely into a shed, but the dingoes were persistent and were standing by, waiting for any opportunity.

Meanwhile, the plight of little 'Ellie' became headline news on the local radio station and had been broadcast locally hoping that somebody maybe able to help.

One of the tourist operators on the mainland had been contacted by telephone and asked to obtain and bring a bag of "Di-vet-a-lac" for Ellie on his run up the beach later that day.

Sonia Hutchinson a horse lover who runs an Arabian Stud had a friend who informed her about Ellie's plight. Sonia being a devoted caring soul immediately rang another friend Bev to start the lengthy process of dealing with all the 'Red-Tape' of the Queensland Parks and Wildlife and the Environmental Protection Agency.

Whilst these Government bodies have made it crystal clear they don't want the valuable rare brumbies on the Island, considering them feral and blaming them for erosion on an island constructed of moving sand (they have eliminated most of them- there is only a dozen or so left), but if you want to take one off. – **Oh! Dearie me! That's another story altogether**.

After many phone calls the ranger reluctantly agreed to issue a permit for Ellie's removal from the island.

Meanwhile the residents of Orchid Beach changed their minds and decided the foal should stay on Fraser Island - as there are so few brumbies left now. They believed she could play a vital role in increasing the numbers should Ellie survive. So that was that – or so we thought…until fate intervened.

Impacted. The loss of the magnificent brumbies their loss equates also to the loss of human safety around dingoes. Photo by Norma Hannant.

*Starving dingo desperate for food (like border security) searches the roof
rack on top of a 4WD vehicle. Photo by Norma Hannant.*

We left it for a day, then rang them again, but they had made a definite commitment to try to rear
Ellie themselves. When the ranger heard about what was happening, and that the foal was still on
the island, he telephoned Sonia and said that: *"if the foal was not removed Ellie will be destroyed"*.

Apparently Queensland National Parks and Wildlife didn't want a hand-reared foal running loose
on the island – so once again we were faced with the logistics of removing her.

Thankfully, a kind-hearted fisherman who was about to leave to take his large ice-box of fish catch
to the market. Offered little Ellie a "possie' in the back of his utility! So with her legs secured she lay
in the utility tray amongst all the fishing gear, bouncing around with that huge esky and assorted
tools, during the long trip down the beach in the hot blazing sun, safe but all alone in the world
without access to her mother's security for protection and her milk to sustain her.

Finally, when they safely reached the barge landing about 90 minutes later, Ellie was lifted out,
legs unstrained and she stood quietly on the stern looking out at the reflections on the wake as the
barge crossed over the water towards River Heads. Imagine, for just a few moments she wandered
back in her mind to her mum, crying in her heart of hearts and wondered if she would ever hear
her call or see her again.

Ellie was now five days old!

Sonia says it brought tears to our eyes, as this brave little foal walked down off the barge especially
when you consider all she had been through in her short little life. Now she had a ticket to freedom
free from the bias and rules of the harsh red-tape bureaucracy of the QPWS and the EPA.

When Sonia saw her, she was so small. She says, *"I picked her-up and placed her in the rear of my
Pajero where she stood ever so quietly looking curiously out the back window. Her little legs were
no-longer shaking with fear"*.

Ellie is now living happily at Walker's Point. Special thanks to Sonia Hutchinson's mercy mission (with help from her loyal friends) and her very kind permission to relate dear Ellie's story.

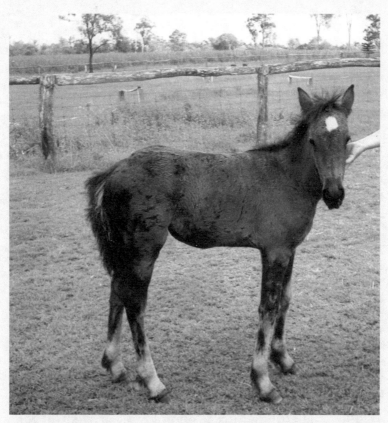

'Ellie' at 6-months of age surviving thanks to her career at Walker's Point. Photo by Sonia Hutchinson.

Did you know, the purest breed of dingoes in Queensland are not as lucky as Ellie? They are playing out a horrific cruel-saga an unquantified number and value. Where the horses were removed over alleged erosion. Now the dingoes were being blamed for so-called 'Aggression' a misnomer for 'Self-Preservation' when dingoes motivated by hunger enter campsites looking for the food they can smell (they are not there for photographs as the manager claims).

Given that the manager (the QPWS) was charged with caring and nurturing for not only the wildlife but protecting visitors and the ecosystem from impacts and harm. Instead what was delivered seemed to be the reverse, killing, removals, starving the dingo, the islands top predator and carnivore of its cardinal food resources and with knowledge exposed the community as a possible prey to receive nips and bites (dFIDMS 1999) Perhaps worst of all their plan claimed *"Dingoes like other dogs are capable of killing people"* (dFIDMS 1999). What follows now is this pure-bred dingo population gene-pool is in chaos, threatened by unviability, unhealthy sand colic, affected animals being forced by starvation and are desperate they have killed a human. There are virtually no horses left to prey-on, forced to consume sand coated fish offal and finally facing extinction. **WARNING!** To my mind over the next ten years dingoes will not exist on Fraser Island anymore; it is also verified according to expert (Dr. Cairns 2016). Soon, international visitors and others will never see the wild pure-bred dingo on Fraser Island again.

Forestry Department 1904 -1978 ran opposing policy to the strategies adopted by QPWS - Forestry fed scraps to the dingoes. Photo taken by author circa 1969 at Central Forestry Station.

The Forestry Department managed Fraser Island successfully from 1904 until 1978 (74+ years) they had few if any attacks from the dingo population, certainly death of a human visitor was totally unheard of. In 1969 the author took a photograph at Central Station of the Forestry Departments policy of feeding food scraps to dingoes.

Hand feeding a dingo. Photo by Norma Hannant

Signs of more and more desperation for food. Photo by Norma Hannant.

It appears strategies over food-web resources combined with changed dingo behaviour began when the 'joint committee of management' (in 1978) interfered with the cardinal high protein food resources (the brumby). Perhaps if the food resource had not been 'interfered' with, it is my opinion (for what it's worth) the horrific tragic savage mauling to death of a 9-year-old-boy Clinton Gage at Waddy Point on Fraser Island in 2001 (under QPWS management) would most likely never have occurred. Political cover-ups were in the air - as **no coronial Inquiry** was ever conducted into the tragic death of the boy. The 'Headlines' on the front page of one newspaper claimed:

The Government Medical Officer claimed *"Boy's wounds horrify doctor"* Dr. Paul Anderson said: *"Clinton Gage had been disembowelled and had his face, neck, lower abdomen and legs mauled… the cause of death is not officially known…"* according to Fraser Coast Chronicle May 2, 2001.

Since QPWS came to manage Fraser Island in 1971 hundreds of visitors have been injured by dingo attacks to varying degrees.

WARNING BELLS – <u>A GONG</u> - HISTORY WILL REPEAT?

Bells were ringing all the way from Uluru, twenty years after Azaria Chamberlain's death According to the Australian May 2, 2001.

"…The then Uluru chief ranger, Derek Roff, had for two years been writing letters to his bosses in Darwin, warning of increasing cheeky, biting dingoes – and of imminent tragedy. His warnings were buried by the Northern Territory Government and only came to light when a copy of Mr Roff's correspondence was anonymously mailed to the Chamberlain's lawyers…"

The Courier Mail claims: **'ONLY A MATTER OF TIME BEFORE SOMEONE IS KILLED'**. The headlines screamed:

A resident of Orchid Beach claimed:

"...We never had a problem with dingoes until National Parks and Wildlife moved into Waddy Point..."

May1, 2001.

WE MAKE THIS CALL! WE BELIEVE WE NEED THE TRADITIONAL OWNERS MANAGING FRASER ISLAND JUST LIKE IN THE SUCCESSFUL AUSTRALIAN 'KAKADU' AND NOW 'ULURU' NATIONAL PARKS MODEL.

As for that pot of gold rumoured at the end of the rainbow, well you may have thought that sand erosion was Fraser Island's greatest enemy (if you listen to the manager), but something else has overtaken, that is far, far worse than erosion:- 500,000+ tourists per annum with their destructive 4WD's and their mother-load of food. Despite best intentions no-one it seems has yet discovered the tragedy that befell the horses and the dingoes under the arc of the rainbow.

Instead, QPWS has left all humanity with a World-Wide legacy of injury, death and environmental destruction on Fraser Island.

Twenty-five years later the dingo has become more desperate and continues to scavenge for a 'sustainable food replacement' daily humans are camped in their territory with a Mother-load of food. Dingoes cannot be blamed they are doing everything to survive using their senses eyes, nose and ears; attempting to make-up for their loss of the high protein food resource - the wild horse.

These two species, were once inexplicably locked in a balanced predator and prey relationship, now the dingoes are sinking their teeth into another thus confirming with every bite - their behaviour change towards humans due to QPWS management plans of 'interference'.

What a catastrophic pity 'Billy the Bushman' a horseman extraordinaire wasn't in charge now, things would be dramatically different for you and me - as he would understand and know what to do (in comparison to F.I.D.O or inexperienced bureaucrats).

After 1971 the Queensland Government seemed to be happy with their development outcome of a forest of extreme harsh management plans, introduced where once <u>no people and dingo plans existed</u> or were even considered necessary it seems.

Adding to that developing catastrophic crisis and their poor-call about removal of rare and highly valuable rare Suffolk Punch horses, in lieu promoting excessive tourism up to 500,000+ visitors per annum. The QPWS have just about tried everything to control the dingo i.e. shooting, impacted food resources, withdrawing access to rubbish dumps, withdrawn access to buried fish offal, put in place fines for visitors feeding dingoes, fenced areas to exclude the dingo.

But what the manager has never done *is restrict the access numbers of 4WD's and numbers of visitors* in any of their forest of plans.

The dingoes are starving as the evidence has shown. Two expert authors claim: ***"Wild dogs simply do not attack humans unless humans have set the scene for this to occur..."*** *'Spirit of the Wild Dog'* Rogers L& Kaplan G, 2003.

Many visitors have been invited by the manager to camp within these starving dingo territories where the top predator is a carnivore on Fraser Island. Most visitors have floor to ceiling a mother-load of food packed tightly into their 4WD's. Many folks also recognise the Manager sure has collected a huge volume of access fees from 4WD operators, but in doing so, swamped Fraser Island's (K'Gari) with up to a million trampling feet and escalating numbers of 4WD's vehicles upon the now damaged, imbalanced fragile ecosystem food-web.

NEGLIGENCE IS RIFE:

Never ever known before in the entire history of Fraser Island, in the non-sensibility stakes it has been recently reported the Queensland Government have had over $6 million in 'negligence' payout claims brought against it to date, not including a massive secret compensation payout to Clinton Gage's family for the savage mauling to death of their precious boy Clinton at Waddy Point in 2001.

Impacted. Ghost Crabs have been 'crushed to shell grit' by massive numbers of 4WD vehicles & eaten by dingoes traveling the beach at night or in early morning hours. Photo by author.

Talking about the wild horses' pivotal and vital role in human safety on Fraser Island Dean Wells Environment Minister in 2014 espouses his poor 'understanding' exclaiming it was a: *"A good result for the horses and a good result for Fraser Island"*

INCOMPLETE LIST

Or was it quite the opposite - a good result for recreational/tourism - a bad result for the island's once magnificent wilderness and erosion, wild horses, blue couch grass, pure-bred dingo, skinks sea bird habitats, beach thicknee, pied oyster catchers, sea eagles, brahminy kites, red-browed finches, bull finches, bush stone-curlews, pythons, and rare ground dwelling birds, recreational fishing, sea snakes, turtles, eugaries, ghost crabs and their nursery habitat, sea worms and essential sea food for the dingo as well as the fragile impacted land ecosystem of Fraser Island or the effects upon the delicate threads of human safety?

To my mind the evidence is overwhelming with over 500 people attacked by dingoes and one death – it seems the visitors are being exposed to extreme danger (and death) by QPWS strategies and a forest of harsh extreme management plans and exposed to the mercy of starving carnivores.

According to two expert authors Managers' it seems have lacked understanding and have attempted to change the scene by using devastating food deprivation (without offering replacements) and like all carnivores the size of a dog or more, they are potentially dangerous to humans. (Rogers & Kaplan 2003). You be the judge!

A flock of Policemen birds impacted, pied oyster catchers prior to QPWS management in 1992. Now reduced to less than a dozen pairs and falling. Photo by author Circa 1970.

As the wind continuously blows the golden sand grains towards the western shore-line, I think of 'Billy the Bushman', a horseman extraordinaire, his bush craft skills and those magnificent horses. I think of dear Ellie an ancient Arab breed foal - the last brumby to escape Fraser Island. I think of *'Nellie'* and *'Laddie'* two favourite Suffolk Punch horses of the 'Epps' and of all that's been lost; rustling fields of golden paper daises, a clear water creek where a giant fern grows tall. Nearby ancient cycads interspersed by lush mare's tail fern surrounded by the seemingly endless perfume of nature's fruits and flowering gifts. I yearn over and over for what's been lost, the horses' mothering foals, timid pretty faced wallaby, the flocks of 'policemen birds' the loss of pied oyster catchers' breeding ground. In my mind I imagine those flocks of such delicate little creatures the red-browed finches flittering around and the way Central Station used to be before QPWS. Missing, the scene in the still of the night, is the endless call of the dozens of bush stone-curlew that used to reside there. As

I'm carried away in my mind's eye I see a grave stone hidden far away in the shadows in the bush marking the distant memory of a pure-bred dingo that one lived on Fraser Island. Nearby a Willy Wag-Tail sitting on a fallen log – she softly tweets as it catches a march fly on the wing, then lands again and is prompted to twist its body, tail erected waving this special memory –of 'goodbye'.

Hidden in the scrub. The grave of the last pure-bred dingo called simply dog. Photo by author.

For further reading see Fred Williams's publications:

1. *'Written in Sand' a History of Fraser Island'* 1982.
2. *'Princess K'Gari's Fraser Island – Fraser Island's Definitive History".* 2002. **Purchase your copy now. Contact _mkrail@bigpond.net.au_ while stocks last.**
3. *'Wangoolba Prince Amongst Dingoes"* Trafford.com 2006.
   Another book unrelated subject written by Fred Williams.
4. *OH! Brother! Against all odds!* Zeus Publications. 2012.
   http://www.zeus-publications.com

NOTE: NEW RELEASE IMMINENT: A series of books on the catastrophic years under QPWS on Fraser Island is planned to be released ASAP, as soon as sponsors' can be finalised. Naming rights are available for this series. If you wish to be involved please contact the author: _vicfred@activ8.net.au_

ILLUSTRATIONS.

The whole is extensively illustrated with an excellent range of historical photographs 70+ it's a virtual exposition of memorabilia, included in the text, some are in mono whilst others are in full colour. A picture they say tells a thousand words, many will find these photographs tell it like it's never been told before that have been sourced from the diverse interest of different creators.

******

(Poem reproduced with the kind permission of the creator.)
OH! DEARIE ME! 'ELLIE'.

The fear was seen in Ellie's eyes
Her mum was spooked and ran away
With biting dingoes on her back
She shook with pain that awful day.

The loving care this story brings
Is worth all the praises it sings
As it lights up 'Ellie's new life
Free from QPWS Strategies 'n' Strife!
....

Brian McClelland 2017.

Ellie as a mature horse. Photo compliments Sonia Hutchinson.

Printed in the United States
By Bookmasters